THE USBORNE

BIG BOOK OF DINOSAURS

Written by Alex Frith

Illustrated by Fabiano Fiorin

Designed by Stephen Wright

Dinosaur expert: Dr. Darren Naish

Meet the dinosaurs

Long, long ago, before there were any people, there were animals known as dinosaurs all over the world. Some of them were very, VERY big.

Dinosaurs were the BIGGEST animals that have ever walked on land.

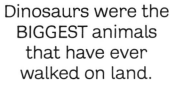

Up in the sky, dinosaurs were watched by flying creatures known as pterosaurs.

No one knows exactly how big the biggest dinosaur was. But it was at least as LONG as a swimming pool, as TALL as three buses, and HEAVIER than twenty elephants.

Dinosaur babies hatched from eggs. They started out no bigger than a chick, but very soon they grew AND GREW AND GREW...

Diplodocus had bumps all the way along its back.

Telmatosaurus teeth were good for grinding up plants to eat.

Tsintaosaurus horns were hollow, so they wouldn't have been too heavy.

Iguanodon had big spikes on its thumbs.

Protoceratops was as big as a VERY big dog.

Supersaurus had a MASSIVE body but a tiny head.

Compsognathus was only as big as a chicken.

Brachiosaurus had a VERY strong heart.

The very biggest dinosaurs

Dinosaurs came in all shapes and sizes. Some were only little, but others were absolutely ENORMOUS.

Lift the pages and see if you can spot all these dinosaurs in the scene underneath.

Compsognathus
0.7m (28 inches) long

Eoraptor
1m (3 feet) long

The VERY biggest dinosaurs are known as sauropods. They had long necks, long tails, and ate plants.

Iguanodon
9m (30 feet) long

Parasaurolophus
10m (33 feet) long

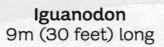

Brachiosaurus
26m (85 feet) long
Brachiosaurus could lift its head as high as six double-decker buses.

Argentinosaurus
37m (123 feet) long
Argentinosaurus probably weighed 100 tonnes (110 tons) – that's more than 16 elephants.

Apatosaurus
23m (76 feet) long

Protoceratops
2m (7 feet) long

Pteranodon
1.8m (6 feet) long
7.8m (25 feet) wingspan

Tsintaosaurus
10m (33 feet) long

Stegosaurus
9m (30 feet) long

Telmatosaurus
12m (38 feet) long

Supersaurus
42m (140 feet) long

Diplodocus
45m (148 feet) long – that's as long
as five buses parked end to end.

Diplodocus

Argentinosaurus

Apatosaurus is sometimes called brontosaurus.

Enormous sauropods could eat all the leaves from a whole tree in a single day.

Eoraptors ate meat.

Up in the air

In the time of the dinosaurs, the skies were full of flying creatures called pterosaurs.

Zhejiangopterus had a very long beak compared to its body.

The largest pterosaur was called **hatzegopteryx.** Its HUGE wings were 12m (39 feet) from end to end. Each wing was taller than a double-decker bus.

Quetzalcoatlus could stretch its wings 10m (33 feet) from end to end.

Tropeognathus had a wingspan of 6m (20 feet).

Tupuxuara had an ENORMOUS crest on its head.

Rhamphorynchus was only as big as a goose.

Anhanguera had long spiky teeth.

Ornithocheirus was 3m (10 feet) tall when it walked on all fours.

Archaeopteryx was one of the world's first birds.

Spinosaurus lived and hunted in rivers.

Giganotosaurus had the biggest head of any theropod.

Triceratops had a MASSIVE head and long horns.

Therizinosaurus had INCREDIBLY long claws.

Little **bambiraptors** hunted in packs.

Spinosaurus had a HUGE sail on its back, for showing off.

Big, scary monsters

The SCARIEST dinosaurs were towering monsters with big teeth and sharp claws.

Even the dinosaurs they hunted looked scary. They were covered in horns, spikes and rocky bumps to protect them.

Lift the pages and see how many of these dinosaurs you can find in the scene underneath.

Troodon
2m (6 feet) long
Ate other dinosaurs

Bambiraptor
0.7m (27.5 inches) long
Ate other dinosaurs

Pachyrhinosaurus
7m (23 feet) long
Ate plants

Triceratops
9m (30 feet) long
Ate plants

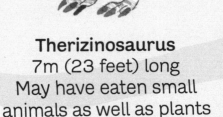

Therizinosaurus
7m (23 feet) long
May have eaten small animals as well as plants

Tyrannosaurus
12.4m (40 feet) long
Ate other dinosaurs

Giganotosaurus
14.3m (46 feet) long
Ate other dinosaurs

Velociraptor
1.8m (6 feet) long
Ate other dinosaurs

Deinonychus
3.4m (11 feet) long
Ate other dinosaurs

Styracosaurus
5.5m (18 feet) long
Ate plants

Pentaceratops
8m (26 feet) long
Ate plants

Sauropelta
7.6m (25 feet) long
Ate plants

Ankylosaurus
10.5m (35 feet) long
Ate plants

Carcharodontosaurus
14m (44 feet) long
Ate other dinosaurs

Spinosaurus
15m (50 feet) long
Ate other dinosaurs

Big, scary, meat-eating
dinosaurs are known as
theropods. Spinosaurus was
the largest known theropod.

Tyrannosaurus had jaws strong enough to crush a car.

Sea monsters

At the time of the dinosaurs, the seas were full of huge, fearsome creatures. Some were as big as whales, but with LONG necks, or MASSIVE, powerful jaws.

Liopleurodon had lots of very sharp teeth.

Fish-eating **mosasaurus** was a 16m (50 feet) monster.

The Jurassic era:
206 – 145 million
years ago.

Rhamphorynchus
lived 150 million
years ago.

Liopleurodon
lived 160 million
years ago.

Stegosaurus
lived 155 million
years ago.

Lightest dinosaur
(0.3 kilos /
0.7 pounds)

Archaeopteryx
lived 145 million
years ago.

Compsognathus
lived 155 million
years ago.

Tallest dinosaur
(18m / 60 feet)

Dinosaur with
the longest neck
(16m / 52 feet)

Supersaurus lived
155 million years ago.

Diplodocus lived 155
million years ago.

Sauroposeidon
lived 150 million
years ago.

Brachiosaurus
lived 150 million
years ago.

Mighty **hainosaurus** ate all sorts of sea creatures.

Elasmosaurus was 14m (40 feet) long. That's a little longer than three cars parked end to end.

Tylosaurus could
leap out of the
ocean to catch
birds in the sky.

Thalassomedon was
12m (40 feet) long.
Its LONG neck was half
of its entire body.

Timeline of dinosaurs

The first dinosaurs appeared about 220 million years ago. But they didn't all live alongside each other. Here are just a few creatures from each time period:

Mixosaurus lived 220 million years ago.

The Triassic era: 248 – 206 million years ago.

Lariosaurus lived 220 million years ago.

Nothosaurus lived 230 million years ago.

Eoraptor lived 220 million years ago. It was one of the very first dinosaurs.

Shonisaurus lived 210 million years ago.

Dinosaur with the longest tail (13m / 42.6 feet)

Mixosaurus was smaller than a person.

Lariosaurus was only half the size of a turtle.

Nothosaurus ate fish.

Shonisaurus was the biggest ancient sea monster. It was 21m (69 feet) long – three times the size of a great white shark.

The Cretaceous era: 145 – 65 million years ago.

Anhanghuera lived 115 million years ago.

Tsintaosaurus lived 75 million years ago.

Iguanodon lived 130 million years ago.

Giganotosaurus lived 100 million years ago.

Sauropelta lived 115 million years ago.

Carcharodontosaurus lived 110 million years ago.

Protoceratops lived 70 million years ago.

Argentinosaurus lived 95 million years ago.

Troodon lived 75 million years ago.

Brainiest dinosaur

Quetzalcoatlus lived 65 million years ago.

Dinosaur with the longest teeth (36cm / 14 inches)

Dinosaur with the longest horns (1m / 3 feet)

Tyrannosaurus lived 65 million years ago.

Triceratops lived 65 million years ago.

Fastest dinosaur (65 km/h / 40 mph)

Ornithomimus lived 65 million years ago.

Elasmosaurus lived 65 million years ago.

Heaviest dinosaur (100 tonnes / 110 tons)

The last dinosaurs died out 65 million years ago.

Dinosaur footsteps

Some dinosaurs have left behind footprints that you can still see today.

The footprints on these pages are shown actual size.

A young **tyrannosaurus** footprint is 46cm (18 inches) long.

An adult **tyrannosaurus** footprint is 83cm (33 inches) long.

The smallest dinosaur footprint that has been found was made by **grallator**. It's 76mm (3 inches) long.

The biggest dinosaur footprints are 1.5m (59 inches) long and 1.2m (47 inches) wide. They probably belong to **brachiosaurus**.

Usborne Quicklinks

For links to websites where you can watch video clips
about dinosaurs and hear how to say all the names in this book,
go to **www.usborne.com/quicklinks** and type in the keywords
"**big dinosaurs**". Please follow the internet safety guidelines
at the Usborne Quicklinks website. We recommend that children
are supervised while using the internet.

Series designer: Mary Cartwright Series editor: Jane Chisholm
Additional design by Lisa Verrall and Laura Wood

Digital design by John Russell

This edition first published in 2017 by Usborne Publishing Ltd., Usborne House, 83-85 Saffron Hill, London EC1N 8RT, England.
www.usborne.com Copyright © 2017, 2010 Usborne Publishing Ltd. The name Usborne and the devices 🏆🎈 are Trade Marks of Usborne Publishing Ltd.
All rights reserved. No part of this publication may be reproduced, stored in a retrieval system, or transmitted in any form or by any means, electronic,
mechanical, photocopying, recording or otherwise without the prior permission of the publisher. First published in America 2010. Printed in China. UE.